NICHOLAS HERD

The Conscious Intersection

A Collection of Mantras & Meditations for Everyday Survival.

Copyright © 2022 by Nicholas Herd

All rights reserved. No part of this publication may be reproduced, stored or transmitted in any form or by any means, electronic, mechanical, photocopying, recording, scanning, or otherwise without written permission from the publisher. It is illegal to copy this book, post it to a website, or distribute it by any other means without permission.

Use what works for you in this book and leave the rest for a rainy day.

First edition

This book was professionally typeset on Reedsy. Find out more at reedsy.com

Contents

I   Dedication.

II   Meditations, Mantras, and Food for Thought.

1	How To Meditate.	5
2	I am not the body, I am not the mind.	7
3	So Ham.	9
4	I am not my thoughts, God lives between my thoughts.	11
5	My mind may travel, but I am still here.	13
6	I am bringing things in, and letting things go. All for the...	14
7	What I am seeking is also seeking me.	16
8	I am not in competition with myself.	17
9	I am not at war with myself.	19
10	Apply pressure with the stillness.	21
11	What's in the way is the way.	23
12	Account for what is known.	25
13	Account for the unknown.	27
14	Account for the tension.	29
15	Account for what is forgotten.	31

16	Remember those who are gone.	33
17	Remember those who are here.	35
18	Meditate on your patterns.	37
19	Scan for truths and lies.	39
20	Swim through your conscious mind.	41
21	M.O.N.E.Y and Currency.	43
22	Sitting with cherished memories.	45
23	Something that is landing on your heart.	46
24	A lawn without humans is grass.	47
25	You are doing something.	48
26	The thing has happened.	49
27	Papa's Desk.	50
28	A gift is a gift.	51
29	New information is made daily.	52
30	A good companion is a good mirror.	54
31	The observer.	56
32	Give so much thanks.	58
III	Thank You.	

I

Dedication.

I dedicate this book to my grandparents.

II

Meditations, Mantras, and Food for Thought.

1

How To Meditate.

The world is busy and full of information. We process a lot of information on a daily basis. Some information is helpful and some information is distracting. Meditations help us focus on what matters in the moment.

When meditating with this book, simply notice your thoughts and notice your breathing as you read. Notice what there is to notice, and try to notice without judgment. If there is nothing for you to notice, then notice that too.

There are many different breathing exercises, but the most important thing is that you allow yourself to keep breathing. If you ever get lost in your mind, use the **mantras** at the top of each page to keep you focused. A mantra is a word or phrase, something like a motto, that you can repeat in your mind to help calm your nervous system. My favorite mantra is, *"Breathing in, I know that I'm breathing in. Breathing out, I know that I'm breathing out."*

When meditating with mantras, it is not important to get the words exactly right. Just feel the vibration of what you are trying to convey.

When meditating, set a timer to monitor your progress. Start with 60 seconds and work your way to higher numbers. Do not judge your process, simply trust it!

2

I am not the body, I am not the mind.

I am not the body, I am not the mind.

There is a silent observer in all of us. There is something that is watching your thoughts and actions, and it is happening from the inside. If you can hear yourself thinking, then ask yourself, "Who is listening to these thoughts?".

Throughout the years the body and mind will change. The mind can receive new information and start to think differently. The body will go through changes throughout the life cycle. Throughout the different changes, you are still you. There is something in you that has been consistently there your whole life.

If you lose an arm, leg, or some other part of your body, you are still whole. If your mind starts to deteriorate, you are still whole. You are an unwavering consciousness that continues on, even after your body has left the earth. You are one with everything. It could be said, you are both the body and the mind, and yet neither at the same time. Sit quietly and observe the parts of you that are alive. Notice them, and find the joy in knowing that they are there. Do not hold onto them, they only need to be acknowledged.

I am not the body, I am not the mind.

3

So Ham.

Inhale "So", Exhale "Ham".

There are many things you can identify with when completing the phrase "I am___". This mantra allows you to let go of trying to create the right answer. In your daily life, attachment to your identity allows it to flourish. Whether it be in career or in relationships, to some degree it is healthy to care about your role in society. You know that you have become overly attached to these identities when you lose your sense of boundaries around them. You were somebody before you accepted the roles you identified with, therefore you have the potential to be something different and possibly greater in the future.

The So Ham mantra acknowledges the infinite potential to be all things. "So Ham" translates to "I am". What comes after that phrase could be many things. For me, "I am" could be followed by an identity such as "father", "brother", "yogi" or "friend". It could be followed by a descriptor; "I am kind" "I am tall" "I am funny". It could be a state of mind; "I am loving", "I am connected", "I am free". The list may be different for the next person, but even if all those things changed, as long as I am alive, then "I am". Your job will change, the relationships you make will change, your own belief system may change, but you will always be you.

Inhale "So", Exhale "Ham".

Time Out:

Either alone or with a partner, ask the question "Who are you?" and see how many answers you come up with. You can set a timer (2-5 minutes) or go to a certain number of answers (25-100).

4

I am not my thoughts, God lives between my thoughts.

I am not my thoughts, God lives between my thoughts.

In between each moment, there is a small gap of empty space. Even in your breath cycle, there is a small gap. Even in your thinking, if you allow it, there is room for this small gap. Take a moment to experience it, and you will see that it is so. You can ask yourself, "What am I going to think about next?", and from that you might notice the gap even more. When you realize you are not your thoughts, you allow them to be more transient and in turn you can be less attached.

In that momentary gap, there is a vastness that holds potential energy. In that gap, there is energy that has not been formed into anything that our minds can imagine. In that moment your ego, or identity, is temporarily free from having to create/say/do anything. Your sense of self is important and a predominant driving force in your life, but for that momentary gap, that force gets to be still.

Your ego is a part of you, and it is trying to create a reality that may come true, but it will also cause suffering. There is a higher intelligence playing some factor in directing your life. When you are not trying to figure things out on your own, you can see the work of this higher intelligence clearly. Whether it is labeled as "God", "Source", "Spirit", or the "Universe", people find solace in knowing they are not alone in guiding their lives. When you experience the gap between your actions, you can witness the quiet force that holds this universe together.

I am not my thoughts, God lives in between my thoughts.

5

My mind may travel, but I am still here.

My mind may travel, but I am still here.

Your mind has the ability to travel thousands of miles and is not bound by linear time. Your body can only travel to one place at a time. Your mind can split off and go in multiple directions. Your body can only be pulled in one direction. Your mind can take you to many places; you can remember great experiences but also relive painful memories. Your body goes one place at a time; it is always in the "now". Whenever your mind creates its own reality, whether it be a wondrous fantasy or dreadful paranoia, if you ever need to bring yourself back to what is happening right in front of you, you can remind yourself that, "Everywhere you go, there you are".

My mind may travel, but I am still here.

6

I am bringing things in, and letting things go. All for the highest good.

I am bringing things in, and letting things go. All for the highest good.

There is a universal exchange happening that allows for creation and destruction. We can see it in our galaxy system, and we can see it in our breathing. A breath enters in and down the body; the diaphragm rises and expands the lung tissue. That breath then exits up and out the body; the diaphragm lowers and contracts. Cells are replenished, new clarity is brought in, and what no longer serves us has been expelled in this cycle of breath. It took both bringing something in and letting something go, for this to happen. There are things we are hesitant to bring in because it will affect what we are used to. Those same things might need to change to usher in what serves us today. In between creation and destruction is growth, and it becomes the foundation for what our next breath, venture, decision is based upon. If we are ever concerned with detaching from the life we knew, we can remind ourselves that every decision we are making, is geared around the *intention* of nurturing what honors our most authentic self.

I am bringing things in, and letting things go. All for the highest good.

Time Out:

What are 3 things that you are bringing in, and 3 things you are letting go of for your highest good?

_____ _____

_____ _____

_____ _____

7

What I am seeking is also seeking me.

What I am seeking is also seeking me.

The goals that you are chasing are not running away from you; they are responding to you. When you put your thoughts, prayers, intentions, and actions in motion, everything in your world is responding to that. There can be roadblocks of all kinds. Family, friends, and even your own internal dialogue can delay the process of meeting your goals, but your dominant intention is still the one with the highest attraction point. Even if roadblocks delay the process, what you are searching for is also trying to find its way through.

For years, feelings of inadequacy delayed my feelings of success. When I finally stood still, I realized the successful feelings I was running from were coming towards me and always had been. Once I let go of the belief of unworthiness, I found things got to me much quicker.

What I am seeking is also seeking me.

8

I am not in competition with myself.

I am not in competition with myself.

The idea of "Me vs Me" is complicated. It has been helpful for many people overcoming self-doubt, self-sabotage, and limiting beliefs. This is certainly a motivating tool, but can also create opposition that doesn't need to exist. Bodies and mindsets change all of the time, and if you continue to move the finish line, you may miss out on actually celebrating your achievements. The word "settling" can seem unattractive, especially for the highly ambitious, but adding a sense of being "content" can be as progressive to your journey as the continuous motivation/austerity/grind that many of us are used to.

Be a cheerleader for yourself, and release identifying as the doubt/sabotage/limiting beliefs you may experience. You were complete and whole before these negative vibrations entered your space, and you are still complete and whole even if they show up from time to time. It doesn't have to be an internal battle of, "Me vs Me". The enemy is not within. With a "You with You" mindset, you will win and not lose.

I am not in competition with myself.

Time Out:

There are many different styles of teammates. If you were going to be the perfect teammate for yourself, what would that teamwork look like?

_____

_____

_____

_____

9

I am not at war with myself.

I am not at war with myself.

Breathe in and breathe out, and see that the body does not want resistance in the flow of breath. The body does not hold animosity against its own life force. Any affliction comes from an outside experience. You can be at war with an outside source, but you can be at peace within. If you are at war with your memories, have unconditional grace for your experience.

You can wish for no ill will to live in your body. You can wish to harbor no resentment, and to no longer identify with the traumas of your past. When you look at your system within, you will see that it wants to bring in life and life force energy. Your internal system wants to be in harmony within. Even if you don't feel it, know the desire lives within.

Though there can be war from the opposition, you are not the opposition within. Though you can be at war with your past, your past is not who you are within. Even when battling afflictions, harbor no anger or resentment towards the self.

Remember you are at peace. You are not at war with yourself. Though the battles outside may enter your life, remember you are at peace within.

I am not at war with myself.

Time Out:

Take a moment in a reclined or flat position and feel your hand on your heart and the other on your belly. Notice the flow of your breath and heartbeat. You will see the body does not want to hurt you. If you surrender, you will not be defeated.

10

Apply pressure with the stillness.

pply Pressure with the stillness.

Anxieties, of all kinds, will play you out of position. In other words, at times you are exactly where you need to be, and worrying/doubt/fear can blind this awareness. You then keep searching for what you are looking for, not knowing that you had it all along. You can talk yourself out of anything, if you talk too much. Desires around jobs, pay-raises, first dates, and much more can be achieved by simply standing solid. If things need to be adjusted later on, that is fine, but first be comfortable in standing in what you want.

Let people respond how they need to! Their discomfort is not always meant to be shared as your own. Using stillness is one way to communicate that you are content in your decision, and you are **enough**. You are enough and you don't need to overthink, over analyze, or over explain. The mind may create attachment to something that happened in the past, or in future scenarios that could be realistic or unrealistic. The stillness keeps you in the present and forces you to see what is, now.

Apply Pressure with the stillness.

Time Out:

Don't confuse "inaction" with "stillness". Stillness is a powerful choice when used wisely.

11

What's in the way is the way.

What's in the way is the way.

Adversity is a part of life. The way we deal with adversity becomes a measure of how we grow as people. You can avoid adversity, but that will only work temporarily. The things getting in the way of feeling whole are there for a reason. Whether you are the reason for a situation or not, if it affects your well being, then it is your responsibility. In many situations, the only way out *is* through.

If you find yourself avoiding something, it is healthy to question why. Some things that you avoid may be the very thing that pushes you to a new level of success. In your careers and in relationships, there will be opportunities to become a better communicator and advocate when you accept the things in front of you as necessary to your growth. For the vast majority of people who find great success in their life, there were moments of adversity that they overcame to get to the next level of understanding.

What's in the way is the way.

Time Out:

Is there something along your journey that you feel is in the way? What will you learn about yourself through overcoming this hurdle?

12

Account for what is known.

When I feel what I have, I have enough. When I use what I have, I have enough.

To account for what is known puts you in a state of grounded awareness. When your consciousness gets stuck in your head, remember that you are on the ground. Your feet, your chair, some part of you is connected to the surface of the earth. Remember that you are on the ground and the tension can go away.

Maybe the sun is shining. Account for that. If you cannot see the sun, know that it is shining somewhere. The moon is in connection with the earth. You yourself are a piece to a larger puzzle. Your presence makes some impact on the world in some way. This is your planet too, and you are allowed to be here! Do your dance and march to the beat of your drum; you have the right to contribute how you see fit.

When you account what for what is known, start with an

emphasis on the what feels "good". "Good" as in feeling whole, supported, and energized to live your life. You know the sun is shining, even when it is hidden on a cloudy day. You know that you have breath in your body and you have a beating heart. You know that if you have nothing else, you have the present moment. In the present moment, even as you read this, you are alive and can find gratitude in that. You might not know exactly what the future holds, but you've survived 100% of every bad day that you have had. Every obstacle, even something like getting out of bed, may have felt extremely difficult, and yet here you are, still striving in some way.

When I feel what I have, I have enough. When I use what I have, I have enough.

Time out:

Make a list of 10 things you can account for in this very moment, no matter how big or small.

_____   _____

_____   _____

_____   _____

_____   _____

_____   _____

13

Account for the unknown.

round my outline, lives the unknown.
Can you imagine 95% of your life is being informed by things you do not know? Account for the unknown. In space, black matter fills the galaxy and most of its nature is unknown. On earth, the subconscious mind controls the majority of human activity. There are functions of your existence that are unknown but still felt.

"Feelings" and "logic" can exist at the same time and be different, so allow one to not change the other. Some things can be felt for unknown reasons, therefore you should not discredit them. What you do know cannot discredit what you don't know, so account and pay respects to that which is unknown.

Connecting to the unknown around you reveals your own personal outline in the universe. Respect that you are in a relationship with a force that you cannot see, hear, or smell but can feel. There are invisible forces holding us together, part of which is unknown.

Around my outline, lives the unknown.

Time Out:

What are 5 things that you know you don't know? And then consider there are things you don't know you don't know.

_____ _____

_____ _____

_____ _____

_____ _____

_____ _____

14

Account for the tension.

Remind yourself of the ground and the tension will go away. Tension is active energy holding itself disproportionately to the area around it. Tension may be holding on for protective and stabilizing reasons, but it usually goes forgotten and lingers. Much of our tension is held for too long, and we forget where the muscles naturally go to rest. Follow the root of your tension and see where it holds the energy. If you find the source of your tension, you give yourself a "consciousness map". If it is in your shoulders, they may naturally drop in thinking of them; the same is true in your jaw, your fist, your forehead, and more. Understanding your engagement with tension gives you choice. You can heal better when you know where you are healing. Acknowledge your tension, and the tension will find some way to drop.

Tension holds itself tight and needs a place to land. Tension needs a place it trusts to relax. In the physical, when the body lays down comfortably, the ground below supports it, and so the body is relaxed. In the mental, trust and safety will ease tense conversations and fears. When your shoulders, jaw, and forehead settle, you also feel a sense of relief. When a tough issue or conversation is resolved, it is possible to feel a physical change as well.

You can relieve personal stress by remembering you are connected. You are the relative of someone whose feet touched the earth. As you feel your feet on the ground you are also sharing ground with everyone else on the planet. So long as your body has a surface underneath, you can settle, or "ground" into that awareness. Your mind could be in the clouds, but your body is still on this earth. You are always on the ground in some form or fashion, rising to the sky without getting stuck in the clouds.

Remind yourself of the ground and the tension will go away.

Time Out:

Sit still for a moment and scan your body from head to toe. Notice any small parts of the body that may be secretly holding any unnecessary tension. Redirect your breath to that area to soften and release the tension.

15

Account for what is forgotten.

The breath is with us at all times, hiding in plain sight.

There are some things in life that you have experienced that you do not remember. There are things that you cannot remember that you did not forget. These experiences still have shaped you in some way, but lie dormant in the field of consciousness. You can be reminded of things you have forgotten, and the experience can be peaceful or violent. Something pleasant that you forgot can bring a smile to your spirit. If something unpleasant is triggered, the memory can bring pain.

As forgotten experiences operate in the subconscious mind, your breath can be disrupted. If you check on your breath, you may find you have been holding it. When you check on yourself, make sure you have everything you need, including the breath. In noticing the breath, you may also notice the heart beating, the muscles and bones holding your body together, and much more. In taking the time to account for what is forgotten, you remember more than you ever knew.

There is so much memory living within you. In looking for what you have forgotten, more information resurfaces to consciousness. No one knows what you may find when you start recalling memories from your subconscious. You may find memories of yourself as a child, experiences in your late teens and 20's, or even knowledge from the lineage of your ancestors. If you are feeling tension mentally or physically and don't fully understand, remember there can be a block that is holding onto a lot of energy. Take time to sit with it and to see it. It may start to soften and shift with the breath.

The breath is with us at all times, hiding in plain sight

Time Out:

Notice the distance between you and the objects around you. Notice the gap between each breath. Notice the emergence of a brand new cycle of breath.

16

Remember those who are gone.

Think of someone in your life who is no longer here, see how they live within you.

When you lose a loved one, their energy as a single form expands into multiple forms. You can now see them in their favorite places, hear them in their favorite songs, smell them in their favorite foods, and feel them when you hold their clothes. When you lose a loved one, their present condition changes to a timeless state. You can remember them when they were at their most vibrant and healthy; you can remember them beyond their last few years. When you lose a loved one, you may be able to recall elements of their smile, voice, scent, and touch that may not have been available when you last saw them. You can take a moment to see the memories they bring up in your heart when their presence comes to mind. You can still witness how present they are in your life.

Think of someone in your life who is no longer here, see how they live within you.

Time Out:

Write a letter to someone no longer present in your life. Let them know how you have been since they have been gone. You can do what you wish with the letter, you are writing it for you.

17

Remember those who are here.

Think of people in your life that you are connected to, energetically.

We are individuals that are interconnected. Even if we are independent, we still come from somewhere. No matter how isolated you may become, you are bound to have some interaction with other people. Even in isolation, your memories recall people who have passed through your life. A part of them is still existing in your consciousness. How do you know it exists? Because it is there!

In day to day life you may not notice all the smiles, frowns, encouragement, and discouragement you have experienced from others, but it still influences your daily patterns. Your confidence, doubt, trust, and beliefs are all connected to the energy of people you surround or have been surrounded by. If you sit quietly, eventually your mind will drift to a conversation or interaction that you had involving another person. See how the exchange plays in your head, notice how it makes you feel.

Think of people in your life that you are connected to, energetically.

Time Out:

Scan your mind for anyone who you can silently forgive. Release any harboring resentment towards that person. Scan your mind for anyone you can have immense gratitude for, and let your gratitude be known.

18

Meditate on your patterns.

Look within courageously, and acknowledge what you can and cannot change.

Patterns influence our actions. There are some patterns that advance you and some that hold you back. Unraveling them will bring peace. Understanding a pattern will open the door to acceptance. To accept oneself is up to you alone.

Only you can fully decide to accept yourself, but you must also be comfortable accepting what you don't fully understand. We all have chains of behavior that are complex, but made from simple decisions. These decisions make up patterns, and are the sum of many small choices that look like one.

As you author your present and speak life into your future, you must have some understanding of the driving factors that influence your decisions. Your patterns need to be aligned with your vision, so they can help rather than sabotage your plans. If you can locate a pattern that does not align with your highest good, you are in a position to make a change. There are some patterns that may not fully change at once. Try to accept this without spiraling deeper into that pattern. In other words, even if you cannot eliminate a harmful pattern right away, you can still choose to not feed it. If you can acknowledge the patterns that do not serve you, you can be compassionate without being submissive to them.

Many patterns may be working well for you, and some you may notice are not. If you take the time to see the small decisions that made these patterns, some of which were not your own, you may come to understand the truth about these patterns. You can either accept the pattern or change it. If you successfully change the pattern, you can be at peace. If you unsuccessfully change the pattern, be at peace with that until you can try again.

Look within courageously, and acknowledge what you can and cannot change.

19

Scan for truths and lies.

What do I think about myself? Is this my authentic reality?

Mental modifications are things that affect your mind, some of which are painful and some painless. Scan the body for them.

Scan for:
Right Knowledge: What do you know about yourself that is true?
Misconception: What do you know about yourself that is a lie?

Right knowledge is where there is truth. You find it in real life, and in sacred texts. Misconceptions are where there are lies. You can find these in half-truths and labels from the outside world.

When you understand who you really are there can be joy, or

at least painlessness. When you buy into an identity that is not truly yours, it will eventually cause suffering. People may have wrongly judged you; do not take on their labels. They may have only gotten the story half-right; do not let their inaccuracy change who you are. Look within. What feels right to you? Take time to be with yourself to understand who you are.

What do I think about myself? Is this my authentic reality?

20

Swim through your conscious mind.

You don't need to tread water, you are the river that flows.

You are a fluid consciousness space. Imagine you are floating in the waters of your mind, and no matter how much you let go you will not drown. Release the excitement of death and know that you will not drown. Bring excitement to the mundane and experience yourself existing.

You can be content with doing nothing, and slowly the ego may create anxiety. It will create worry just so that the mind can keep on thinking. The ego does not want to die, and yet it will hold your peace hostage with unlikely scenarios. Your conscious mind can expand in infinite directions and create many scenarios, and yet you have not truly gone anywhere. You have truly left nowhere, and are still right here in the "now". Take the fear of drowning away. You do not have to tread water. You do not have to move constantly. You can allow yourself to float until it is time to swim.

You don't need to tread water, you are the river that flows.

Time Out:

Let your mind relax from worrying about "doing" anything. What are the first things that come into or leave your mind?

21

M.O.N.E.Y and Currency.

My energy is currency.

A popular acronym for M.O.N.E.Y is *My Own Natural Energy Yield*. The belief here is: What you put into something will affect what comes out. In our world, money, or currency, is important but overly coveted. The ability to access currency is a legitimate worry for many people. You create a more balanced relationship with money when you can trust your energy is connected to currency. Look at "currency" as an energy "current" that allows things to flow.

Currency allows things to flow, and your energy is connected to the flow of your currency. When your energy is focused and unobstructed, your relationship with currency will change.

Just as a current flows freely when unobstructed, you can imagine your energy in a similar way. If there is something blocking the flow of your energy, the obstruction must be addressed for it to move. Obstructions can appear as many different things, but if you can remove them, you help the flow of energy.

You should receive the currency that is matching your energy. Even though it is not guaranteed, you can still welcome it into your life. Money is one of the ways we refuel and revitalize. It is one of many ways to exchange energy as currency. If you are resistant to working, the money cannot flow with that resistance. If you are too guarded with money it will consume your energy, creating jealousy and greed. Continue to have a healthy relationship around your true needs and desires, and focus your energy into supporting that. Stay consistent, diligent, and adaptive. Share from a place of love, put your best effort into your goals, and continue receiving the currency available to you because of how you use your energy. It may not happen all at once, so practice welcoming every blessing that comes your way. Whether it be in gifts, resources, or fiat currency, trust that your input is speaking to your output.

My energy is currency.

Time Out:

Rub the hands vigorously, then let the hands go still. Feel the energy in your palms and let it flow through your body. Imagine the energy in your hands will create opportunities for currency to come to you.

22

Sitting with cherished memories.

I allow myself to feel.

Sitting with cherished memories can have beauty in it that is joyful, sad, and also appreciative. Allow your mind to wander through a happy memory. What you feel may surprise you.

I allow myself to feel.

Time Out:

Set a timer, turn on some happy/peaceful music/tones, and relax. Notice the sounds, smells, tastes, and feelings you can remember.

23

Something that is landing on your heart.

I am capable of facing what is in front of me.

Sit with something, for 2 minutes or more, to see what is landing on your heart. It may be something that was so small yet so touching, it could have a positive or negative connotation. Notice the density of the sensation landing on your heart. Is it light or heavy in this moment?

I am capable of facing what is in front of me.

24

A lawn without humans is grass.

A *lawn without humans is grass.*
When the grass grows, the lawn needs to be cut. This is because of you, and not because of the grass. The grass does not need itself to be cut, <u>you</u> need the grass to be cut for your reasons. Isn't it amazing that grass has grown? Let's not forget that grass in itself is a beautiful design of life. When the world creates its expectations, we shape ourselves to appear like a lawn. We generally want to present ourselves as taken care of; to be cleaned and groomed in some way. Following the form or not, it is amazing that you are here. Your existence in itself is amazing. Your design is highly intelligent and keeps you together in every way. Even if you grew yourself wild like the tall grass, you are still a beautiful and acceptable creation.

It is fun to arrange and organize, but we must not forget to enjoy all that exists. The grass grows. That is the gift.

A lawn without humans is grass.

25

You are doing something.

You are doing something and have done something.

When we get too caught up in trying to predict the future, anxiety rises and we get stuck in our head. Remember that you are doing something. Even if there is something you need to do, remember that there are things that you have done. Do what must be done, but do not forget your journey.

The thing that you are doing now was birthed from the many steps you have already taken. At this moment, you may be thinking about what you will do next, but you have also done something to get to this point. Celebrate each step of the way, even the missteps.

You are doing something and have done something.

26

The thing has happened.

All around us the thing that needed to be done has happened. The sun has already started shining. The moon and the tides have communicated. The heavens and the stars have communicated eons ago. Only a small part is needed on your end to move the world forward, and most of it is there because you desire it to be. You and your "ego" do have a life to live, so there is work to be done. In loosening your attachment to the ego, you can see much of what you seek is already available. Happiness, and being present, come from within. Do not notice what makes you happy, notice where happiness lives within you. From that source you can inspire more of it into your field. You can celebrate what you desire as something that fuels your happiness. The essence of the desire is happiness, and it existed before you knew it did.

All around us the thing that needed to be done has happened.

27

Papa's Desk.

I love you for not only what you are, but who I am when I am with you.

These were words that I read in a note from my grandpa that I found on his desk after he passed away. Academically he was a teacher, professor, thinker, and writer. Personally, he was Papa. On his voicemail he said an inspirational quote, so if he missed your call you still walked away uplifted. How you make people feel is more lasting than what you said or did. We cherish those that make us feel our best when we are with them. Some people you love don't make you feel the best, but you love them despite it. I hope you all have at least one person who makes you feel your best too.

I love you for not only what you are, but who I am when I am with you.

28

A gift is a gift.

A gift is a gift.

A gift has value. The person giving the gift determines the value, but so does the person receiving it. A person can determine a gift is useful or useless, but the gift itself will still have value. If it is not valued in the same regard between two people, it does not mean the gift isn't worth what you feel it is. The opinions of others do not change the offering as being something divinely created.

A gift is a gift.

29

New information is made daily.

Stay fluid with your self-image, new information is made daily.

Stay fluid with your identity. You can rely on your core principles, but your belief system may change. Your experience shapes your perception, and your perception shapes your reality. If you have a new experience, your perception may change. Our perceptions adapt from life's changes, which also includes trauma. The eyes you see yourself with have seen trauma, so there is a lot to factor in when seeing oneself.

You also may see yourself inaccurately based on misconceptions. I have a friend who was labeled as having a mental disability. In actuality, he was deaf and could not hear the lesson plans. He thought he was stupid and people would call him that. He believed it too, until he learned that he was actually deaf. When he started getting help with his hearing, he became much more confident and went on to live a great life. There is still much to discover about yourself, so you can continue to let your identity evolve.

Stay fluid with your self-image, new information is made daily.

Time Out:

What was a misconception about yourself that you used to live with? What felt real to you about your identity that now appears differently?

30

A good companion is a good mirror.

A good companion is a good mirror.

When going through life, it can help to have a good mirror. When it comes to friends, a good mirror is someone who lets you see your true self. A good friend will allow you to see yourself. If you had dirt on your face, the mirror would show you. If you were looking good, the mirror would show you. Whether you were living in your highest power or not, a good mirror would reveal the truth.

You wouldn't go to a circus-fun-house mirror to get an accurate picture of yourself. That mirror would show you in a distorted light. In a similar sense, you shouldn't go to people who do not truly understand you and expect to get a true reflection of yourself. Even your own mind can trick you into a false identity of self. A good mirror will show you how you are, and present you in your truest light.

To be good mirrors, there must be honesty in the communication. This takes strength on both sides. If you are not living up to your best truth, your mirror should be able to reflect that information to you. At the same time, if you are feeling self-doubt, your mirror can show you that you are perfectly capable of accomplishing your goals. A good mirror is a companion that lets you see yourself.

A good companion is a good mirror.

31

The observer.

Inhale "I", Exhale "Am".

The shadow self told the light self, "I AM". The light self told the shadow self the same thing. The observer watched and listened, and did not learn nor forget...

There is a source of light that shines on you, literally and metaphorically. There is a light that shines on the objects of the world, and there is the illumination of spirit that is present in all living beings. In both cases the light creates a shadow. Even if you think there is no shadow, it is still present somewhere. For every object that has light cast upon it, there is darkness close by. At the same time, even in complete darkness, one can still close their eyes and mentally see the light.

Life has a balance to it. There is yin and yang, and there is cause and effect. Any action done has a shadow side to it. Shadow work is full of things that live under the surface. What lies underneath is a part of your makeup. On this earth everyone has some "good" and "bad". You can honor both with your acknowledgment.

The observer is the part of you that watches. It is in a sense timeless, and watches without judgment, input, or form. The ego, mind, and body all interact with the world we live in. The part of you known as the silent observer simply watches it all unfold. There is nothing for the observer to learn, teach, remember, or forget. The observant self is unchanging and whole, and can be found in the quietest places. When you find stillness, the observant self is more apparent. It is believed by many that this is where our timeless world exists.

Inhale "I", Exhale "Am".

32

Give so much thanks.

There is an endless supply of gratitude available for me and you.

It's risky to say "always" or "never", but you can always find room for gratitude somewhere in your life. There is usually never enough gratitude to go around. Spending time being grateful can happen in as little as one word: "Thanks". Give thanks! Whenever you can. It almost doesn't need much explanation.

One day after picking up my son from school, I purchased him some fries at a drive-thru restaurant. I handed him the fries and as we drove off I asked him to name one person that he could thank for his fries. He thought for a moment and said, "McDonald's". He is a very polite child who says "please" and "thank you" as it is, but his answer made me stop and think of all the workers in the building. His answer made me think of the manufacturers who deliver the food, even the potatoes for being grown. Even with a fast food restaurant, there was room for the sacred ritual of gratitude. This exchange of hot fried potatoes was a small part of the microcosm of people who are all connected at an intersection in the Universe to make this moment possible.

As we find ourselves at an intersection in our own journey together, dear reader, I want to thank you too.

There is an endless supply of gratitude available for me and you.

III

Thank You.

Thank God. Thank you to Mom and Pops. Thank you to all the friends and family. Thank you to Saginaw, NYC, and the Running River Collective. Thank you to the mystical bond that keeps us all together.

www.ingramcontent.com/pod-product-compliance
Lightning Source LLC
Chambersburg PA
CBHW020336010526
44119CB00001B/4